L.D. ROBINSON

D1562993

UNPINNING FEAR
IN EXCHANGE
FOR POWER+

OTHER THOUGHTS
FROM THE 'BOOK

Reading for the Whole Person

INSPIRED published by
Ladero Press LLC
915 Doyle Road, Suite 303, Box #101
Deltona, Florida 32725

First Ladero Press Printing, October 2022

ISBNs
978-1-946981-88-2 Paperback | 978-1-946981-89-9 EPUB
978-1-946981-90-5 Kindle | 978-1-946981-91-2 Audiobook

The Inspired logo is a trademark of Ladero Press.
Library of Congress information available upon request. www.laderopress.com

Facebook is a registered trademark of Facebook, Inc

Victoria's Secret and FEARLESS are included under fair use and permission.

Dedication

In memory of my grandmother
Lula Mae Robinson, née Claitty
"Muh"

There is a special place in the hearts of grandchildren
for good grandmothers.

I was blessed with three wonderful grandmothers, and the
space left by your transition is felt deeply every day.

From phone calls of "Muh, how do you make . . .?" to our
evenings watching some of your favorite gameshows and
hearing, "Londa, you should go on there!" and most
preciously, our time spent taking in God's Word together
and talking about His goodness, I am profoundly shaped
and forever grateful by your presence in my life.

Thank you for being my grandmother.

Table of Contents

Preface

The *Unpinning Series* began as I thought about something one of my grandmothers, my mom's mom, known as "Granny" to her grandchildren, told me about safety pins. She informed me about the value of keeping safety pins for an emergency. It has proven to be true; safety pins are certainly useful in many situations and for many reasons.

The first book, *Unpinning Safety in Exchange for Courage+ Other Thoughts From the 'Book*, provides readers and listeners with the concept of safety pins jammed onto a single safety pin (our lives), and how we sometimes try to make more fit—steadily trying to get the safe cover to close—to no avail. We are encouraged to exchange safe living for a courageous life in which we make room—sliding things out of the way—for what will help us, bless us, nourish us, sustain us, and allow us to plant healthy, life-giving seeds in the lives of others.

This book, *Unpinning Fear in Exchange for Power+ Other Thoughts From the 'Book,* is for the person who needs to address fear in order to make progression in their lives. It is also for the person who feels powerless in the face of life's circumstances, who doesn't feel loved or believes they do not have the capacity to love, and for the person who struggles with being mentally stable enough to function with purpose in life.

2 Timothy 1:7 NKJV tells us, *For God has not given us a spirit of fear, but of power and of love and of a sound mind.* God offers us something wonderfully fulfilling in exchange for the emptiness of fear. He offers us the ability to be all that He is: powerful, loving, and stable.

Many of the entries are those I have written on Facebook on my personal or author page; other content is new. May you be encouraged as you read this second installation of *Unpinning* to unpin fear and take up God's great exchange.

Maitland, Florida
8.28.22

Introduction

Sometime ago, I was invited to minister at Destiny, the women's ministry at a church pastored by friends of our family. While preparing for the Tuesday night session, Father God led me to 2 Timothy, Chapter 1, Verse 7. In obedience, I went to it and read it. This scripture is one that I have known by memory for several decades, as it was one of the first scriptures that I was taught in the early 1980s when my parents, my siblings, and I started attending a new church. It reads as follows:

For God hath not given us the spirit of fear; but of power, and of love, and of a sound mind. (KJV)

He told me to read it, then He told me to re-read it. In doing so, He told me this:

*Londa, I offer a **3-for-1 exchange** when you decide to let go of fear or refuse its attempts to take up residence in your* *life. I offer the spirit of power. I offer the spirit of love. I offer a sound mind.*

As I began to meditate on what He shared with me, I thought about the number of different ways in which fear attempts to attach itself to our lives. Neglect. Rejection. Abuse. Violation. Betrayal. Comfort. Yes, comfort. Oh, there are more ways; these are just *some* of the ways fear tries to take up residence.

If you are challenged by fearful thoughts and imaginations, I believe that this book will empower you to live out your God-given ability to be free, offered by the sacrifice of His son, Jesus.

Living in fear or under the oppression of fear is the operation of Satan and his demonic team. You do not have to be harassed by fear. It is my prayer that this book will cause you to be "strengthened with might in your inner man [i.e., your spirit] by God's own Spirit" (paraphrased from Ephesians 3:16) so that you take your place of partnership in God's plans and *His* thoughts for your life as Jeremiah 29:11 tells us:

11 For I know the thoughts that I think toward you, says the Lord, thoughts of peace and not of evil, to give you a future and a hope. (NKJV)

11 For I know the plans I have for you," declares the Lord, "plans to prosper you and not to harm you, plans to give you hope and a future. (NIV)

11 For I know the plans I have for you," says the Eternal, "plans for peace, not evil, to give you a future and hope— never forget that. (The Voice)

May you never forget that God has not planned a life of fear for you. He has planned a life that, while challenging at times, is still one in which we can take Him up on His promises. May you always remember that what He desires for you is a life of filled with the spirits of "power, love, and a sound mind." You have the opportunity to choose to partner with Him in His plans for your life.

Space has been left throughout the book for you to capture your thoughts as you read the selections. Many a time, I have revisited something I previously read and discovered notes on my thoughts in that moment--something that was given to me for remembrance. Don't miss your thoughts. Don't miss the downloads that I believe will come to you. #DontMissYourMoment

UNPINNING FEAR IN EXCHANGE FOR POWER+

Fearless and Fear LESS

Sometimes, a matter comes down to do or don't. I choose or I don't choose. No fuzzy confusion.

Today, I was getting ready to select a perfume and decided to choose *Fearless* by Victoria's Secret. When I purchased it, the first thing that caught my attention was the name. Not the bottle. Not the brand. The name. I thought, "One has to feel powerful putting this on. Gets the whole mind right." So, some days when I am feeling a bit more pressure to meet deadlines or thoughts come that are contrary to The Eternal One's proclamation, I choose *Fearless* to help me remember throughout the day that every day is a choice to be "Fearless" and to choose to "Fear LESS" every day.

Black and white in photography has often been used to highlight certain things while shadowing others. While taking this picture today to practice black and white photographs, I noticed that there were always shadows from the lighting. Thoughts of fear are like that—lurking and lingering so that we don't find the right space so that we stand in relief. Relief to stand out in our purposes. Relief to stand free from "I can'ts" "This won't evers" and all the other thoughts that want to stop us from becoming and being and doing what we were created for in this life, on this side. Just as it took a few shots to get *Fearless* to show up in the photograph, it may take a few shots for what we're becoming and doing. We must choose to not quit. As Wayne Gretzky stated, "You miss 100% of the shots you don't take!"

Be fearless.

Fear LESS.

Stand out from fear.

Stand in your purpose, your passions, and your pursuits.

You are worth it.

For God has not given us the spirit of fear; but of power, and of love, and of a sound mind. 2 Timothy 1:7 KJV

#Fearless #FearLESS #EverydayChoices

Thoughts on Being Fearless

There are areas in our lives where we stand boldly and others in which we are challenged. Being honest about where we are challenged to operate powerfully, lovingly, and stably helps us to eradicate fear in those areas. For example, some people are bold at work, but feel powerless in their marriages and/or other relationships/engagements outside of work.

Use the space below to capture your thoughts on how you can take steps to become fearless and fear less.

_____

_____

_____

_____

_____

_____

_____

_____

_____

_____

_____

_____

Let's Believe!

Y ou may have heard that the opposite of faith is fear. I'd like to challenge that, if I may.

If faith is believing that what we cannot see in the natural is still possible and can happen, then the opposite of that is this: believing that what we see will not change. If faith is believing that things CAN change, then not believing— unbelief, doubt—is its opposite, its "Consistent Challenger."

Faith says, "I'm starting a new business."

Doubt says, "You can't start a new business."

"Somebody else already has a business like that."

"Why do you want to do THAT?"

Notice, doubt hasn't even given reasons. It just starts questioning your faith!

Fear comes by to drop off all the reasons why--reinforcing doubt's position. May I suggest that you park them both at the curb to be picked up and hauled off?

Fear comes by to see if it can get us to feel powerless, operate in hatred (of ourselves and others), and to make us confused. 2 Timothy 1:7 KJV tells us, *For God hath not given us the spirit of fear; but of power, and of love, and of a sound mind.* Interestingly enough, the juxtaposition of "God not giving us the spirit of fear" is explained by what Paul tells Timothy what God DID give him and very distinctly by the use of "and"—helping us to realize that what God gives is always greater than what fear offers up. We're encouraged to walk in power, AND in love, AND be of a sound mind. Fear is doubt's tagalong, and both are very persistent.

Faith has a consistent challenger named doubt.
Doubt has a bestie named fear.

What will you believe?
Will you choose to walk in power?
Will you choose to walk in love towards God, yourself, and others?
Will you choose to keep a sound mind?

It's a daily calibration activity.

Daily, we have to calibrate our minds to faith's possibilities, choosing to believe in God's goodness towards us and that alone.

Mark 9:23 says, *Jesus said unto him, If thou canst believe, all things are possible to him that believeth.*

Let's make faith big and bold in our lives, giving no space to doubt.

Let's believe!

#LetsBelieve #WhatFaithIs

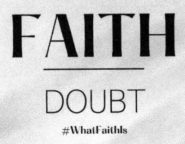

Thoughts on Faith and Doubt

What are some things or areas of your life in which you need to let faith stand big and bold? What can you not see in the natural that your faith needs to manifest for you?

_____

_____

_____

_____

_____

_____

_____

_____

_____

_____

_____

_____

_____

_____

_____

_____

_____

_____

Not Trying Is
Not an Option

Good morning!

Whatever it is that you've been thinking is a good idea, a good product, a good business, or a good cause, you should know this: the idea was provided to you for a reason. You owe yourself a reason to try.

Yes, it may take some work, but if you and your ideas aren't worth the work to YOU, why should others think otherwise?

There is a difference between having a fear of failure and having a fear of trying. While the former group has its own issues, I'd most certainly rather not be in the latter. "I owe it to me to at least try." Interestingly enough, I'd thought about this after a conversation I had yesterday. I was led to

Jonathan McReynolds, Christ Rep.'s song "Try"—check it out.

Be Encouraged! 💙💙💙💙💙

#NotTryingIsNOTAnOption

Night Vision

Genesis 1:14-19 (*The Voice*)

God: *14-15 Lights, come out! Shine in the vast expanse of heavens' sky dividing day from night to mark the seasons, days, and years. Lights, warm the earth with your light. It happened just as God said. 16 God fashioned the two great lights—the brighter to mark the course of day, the dimmer to mark the course of night— and the Divine needled night with the stars. 17 God set them in heavens' sky to cast warm light on the earth, 18 to rule over the day and night, and to divide the light from the darkness. And God saw that His new creation was beautiful and good. 19 Evening gave way to morning. That was day four.*

Yesterday evening, before I left home, I snapped a picture of the night sky. It was beautifully clear. For about a week or so, we (these living souls on Earth) have been able to see the entire solar system. Some planets with the naked eye; others, some assistance is required.

Within an hour or so, I was at the home of my brother and sister-in-love. Shortly after parking on the street, I saw a meteor streak across the sky—a burst of light that was completely unexpected.

After my sister-in-love and the girls arrived, my 4-year-old niece pulled out a solar system project that I'd purchased as a project for us. Before we started, I took her outside to see Jupiter and Saturn. In just under an hour, the night sky had changed. We couldn't see the moon, Jupiter, or Saturn! It was cloudy.

As we worked on a project with some help from Google images pulled up on the TV so that she could clearly see the planets, spell them, and write the names on the back of the models, it was clear how the Sun in our solar system provides much light—even in the vast, seeming darkness of the Milky Way galaxy that contains our solar system. The Milky Way that is only defined by the night sky. Takes shape—with its billions (estimated to be between 100 and 400 billion) of stars. Stars that shine, giving light.

While we frequently rejoice in the sunny days of life—we can see a lot more clearly, things seem closer—we still have to have night vision. When I read Genesis, I was enlightened about how God watched to see that the day light (not daylight) and the night light (not nightlight) performed according to what He'd said—what He'd commanded. He spoke. He watched.

God watched during the night to ensure that the day light came on the scene. He had night vision. However (In which ever way—*literary license used here*) the day light and night light came on the scene, He waited and watched to see that what He'd said would come to pass. *And God saw that His new creation was beautiful and good. 19 Evening gave way to morning.*

Even in the midst of dark days—and, if you live long enough, you are sure to have some days that appear bleaker than others—you got to have night vision, too. Gotta be able to SEE that the dark days will give way to the brighter days. The tough days will give way to less-challenging days.

It takes faith and patience. Faith being the confidence that what you've spoken—just like your Creator—will come to pass in this natural realm. Patience—just like your Creator—to wait and watch through the night for day to come on the scene.

Be encouraged. Instead of speaking fear and doubt during the night, begin or continue to speak the positive, powerful, loving, and sound things that you really desire. Wait and watch. Sharpen your night vision. Day is coming.

L.D. Robinson
11/19/2020
#NightVision L.D. Robinson
#DontMissYourMoment

Fear Comes to Take Up Residence, But Not Here!

NEWS FLASH: God does not have to tear up your house, destroy what you've worked for, or cause fear in you and/or your children in order to get your attention. He can simply speak to you. He has already told us the source of these destructive actions: the devil. Yes, there is one. IF your attention is turned to God in the midst of or after "stealing, killing, or destroying" (John 10:10), then I pray it is because you recognize God's grace—for it could have been you. Maybe you're saying, "But it WAS me!" Evidently, it was not unto your death since you're reading this post, so please be encouraged, YOU can go at it again. It may feel like you will not be able to go on. You may even feel that you would have rather died, but please understand that you CAN go at it again.

While we see natural, elemental things taking place, please understand that it is because we are in a natural realm. No one part of this earth goes without dealing with something—

because it's part of this life . . . that dealing with something. The island that missed the last ten hurricanes may have experienced one this time. Yet, it missed the last ten, while another island had to live out the experience. Still, for both, there was grace.

Because of work travel, I have experienced major earthquakes, blizzards, tornadoes, hurricanes, flooding, and other natural happenings. The OPPORTUNITY to be afraid over the years has been plentiful—from natural things to vehicle break-ins to any number of other things. Yet, I decided that I couldn't afford to be afraid. Why? This scripture I remembered from my parents teaching us as children: *God has not given me the spirit of fear, but of power, and of love, and of a sound mind.* (2 Timothy 1:7 KJV)

I have kept this scripture close to my heart. For fear comes and wants to set up residence in our lives, but we must make a decision EACH time that it cannot stay. As my dad says, "Wrong address! Not here!"

So, as you're taking in news of Irma (and don't take in too much), please do not take in fear. As you're preparing (for "wisdom is the principal thing" Proverbs 4:7), please do not take on panic or anxiety. These things come not just to be temporary for and *in* the storm, but permanent fixtures in your life. We can rebuild homes and offices more easily than rebuilding fearful and anxious minds.

Today is a good day to remind you that You. Are. Loved. Yes, YOU! 🩶🩶🩶

Written in response to a major storm in Florida. No title provided on original post.

Thoughts on Anxiety and A Sound Mind

For the first time in 2021, I experienced an anxiety attack. It was about something that happened years ago, but in that moment the realization of it seemed to overwhelm me. I literally went home and got in the bed. The good news is that I didn't stay there. I put into motion the very things that I have written about in this book. Our minds are precious to God. He has given them to us for our own free choice, not to be dominated by anyone or anything other than our acceptance of His great love and compassion for us. God desires us to be stable, sound in our minds. If there are any areas in your life in which you need to identify anxiety—situations, people, places or things that make you anxious (of great unease), write them down here, and make a decision that they will no longer have a hold on you.

_____

_____

_____

_____

_____

_____

_____

The Screenplay of Your Life

Inspired by the impressive resume posted on an actress's page. I thought, "This is a great example of how to keep stretching the boundaries."

It's your life. Yes, YOUR life. There are enough things that will show up in life that you would never expect. The unexpected transition of a loved one. The unexpected loss of income. The unexpected end of a relationship. Traumatic acts perpetrated by others. You may not expect it, but know this, you still need to SHOW UP! Work your way through the unexpected so that you can continue in purpose.

Don't expend energy you need for the unexpected by not preparing, being bound by fear, wondering what "they" will think, and all the other negative things the enemy throws at your mind and in your way in attempts to get you to not live on purpose and with purpose.

You were created to do something awesome with your time on this side of eternity! "God has deposited a piece of eternity [of Himself] on the inside of you that He expects you to deliver in time [your lifetime]." ~ Dr. Myles Munroe

For a number of years, I told my family, "I love you on purpose and with purpose." Life has many twists and turns . . . come what may, you still gotta do this life on purpose and with purpose.

Yes, You Can!
Don't Miss Your Moment!

#DontMissYourMoment   #KeepShowingUpForYourLife
#LiveOnPurposeandWithPurpose

A title was added to this entry, although no title was provided on original post.

Thoughts on Showing Up in the Movie of Your Life

No one else can show up for your life like YOU! Where have you not been present as you should to realize the outcomes that you desire? Don't let fear keep you from showing up!

_____

_____

_____

_____

_____

_____

_____

_____

_____

_____

_____

_____

_____

_____

_____

_____

_____

Lost in
the Crowd

Write your story. Live it out every single day. The successes. The tries that didn't yield the desired results, but you got the lessons.

It takes courage to write your story—with all the twists and turns that are inherent in life and when the vision seems far larger than what you think you can accomplish. In the words of the famous photographer Gordon Parks, "People could do many things if they just tried, but they're afraid ... At times, I have been afraid, but I have never allowed fear to stand in my way."

Whatever you do, don't get lost in the crowd! Crowd chatter is just that. Chatter by folks in the crowd. Let the vision you have for your life cause you to be just that kind of different so that they wonder, "What's wrong with her?" "What's he up to now?"

Be courageous. Sometimes, things "look crazy on an ordinary day" (a lil' Pearl Cleage) and most certainly to ordinary, crowd-pleasing thinkers. Those with the petty things of their youth: the petty gossip, the petty cliques— just the pettiness. The environment in which you fertilize your dreams matters. If you allow contamination, be courageous, and get it out. It might take some time to uproot it, but don't quit.

At a recent homegoing for the delightful Mrs. Ella Walton, her brother-in-law stated, "I don't have to eulogize Ella. She lived her eulogy." That statement has been added to my life. "*Live* your eulogy, Londa."

Will history know where to look for you, or will you be lost in the crowd?

#LostintheCrowd

Thoughts on Design and Decontamination

Each of us has been designed for great things, respective to God's plans *and* purposes for our lives. His design is one in which we have an opportunity to live out His design and decontaminate the soil in which His design and our dreams are fertilized. Who have you been created to be? What have you been created to do? How do you need to decontaminate your environment so that your soil is rich and conducive to you not getting lost in the crowd?

_____

_____

_____

_____

_____

_____

_____

_____

_____

_____

_____

_____

_____

Dream Big

The other day, I was holding Elle my 10-month-old niece. I like to share music with children. Music teaches so many things. Ava, her 4-year-old sister, and I rock out to "Open Door Season" because it teaches her that she doesn't have to be scared. There's power in what we listen to, and this is very important for kids.

Well, I was randomly singing to Elle while she was waiting on the good grits her mom was cooking for her when these words began to come out of me. I played the song in the car while the girls were on the way home with me.

Upon hearing the song over the radio, Ava asked, "What song is that?"

"A song I sang to Elle today."

"Well, you didn't sing it to me."

"Do you want me to sing it to you?"

"Yessss," she responded softly.

So, I did.

"Dream: A Lullaby for Auntie's Babies"

Dream big

Dream wide

Dream tall and tall and tall

Dream big

Dream wide

Dream tall and tall and tall

You can be anyone you want to be

You can do anything you want to do

You can make a difference in the world

You can make a difference in the world

Words by L.D. Robinson

Just in case you may be one in need of a reminder, #DREAM big! You can make a difference 💜💜💜

DREAM

A Lullaby for Auntie's Babies

L.D. Robinson

Thoughts on Dreaming Big

Write down the biggest dream you have! Don't let fear
keep you from writing it down. Write it down!

_____

_____

_____

_____

_____

_____

_____

_____

_____

_____

_____

_____

_____

_____

_____

_____

_____

_____

_____

The Power of Your Voice: Authenticity

After having lunch with a great guy friend of mine, we went to a nearby music shop. He is a musician, and I've always wanted to learn to play an instrument. While thinking about this desire of mine, I had an epiphany, *Londa, you play an instrument. You play the tambourine!*

Well . . . I was thinking more of the piano. I have always wanted to play the piano (and the drums). We went into the keyboard room; I whipped out my piano app to show him what I could do. He watched me go through a few chord lessons in the app, and then he shared some things with me after we transitioned to the guitar room. While demonstrating some things to me on the guitar, he inquired of me. "What does music mean to you?"

"Music is the soundtrack to my life. Whatever season I'm in, there's always a song, I think, that expresses that season to me. Even when I write fiction, there's a playlist to the story. Sometimes, the music drives the story. Other times, I think, 'There's a song for this chapter!' There's not much I do without music."

"So, what you're saying is that you are able to express your voice. I ask everyone [who wants to play an instrument] this question because it is important to know why. Some people will connect with what you're expressing. Others will not. You have to know how to manipulate the music to express what you want. What you play will not be for everyone, but it will be for someone."

We began to talk about the essence of authenticity, and how important it is to be authentically ourselves, regardless of life's circumstances. When it comes to fear and *fears*, we have to be authentic, as well.

God offers us the spirit of power in exchange for fear, and authentically, we have to recognize what we're facing so that we can triumph over it. While we are encouraged to "call those things which be not as though they were" (Romans 4:17 KJV), we are not called to say that things that exist do not. There is a difference. The former "calling things that be not as though they were" is the operation of God's speaking power, His voice, His creative ability in us.

Because we have been made in His image and likeness, we can speak to circumstances and see them change. When will they change? He did not promise us *when* we would see the change, just that are we are to be like ". . . God who gives life to the dead and calls into being things that were not" (Romans 4:17 NKJV), getting His God-kind of outcomes.

The latter is lying (saying that something does not exist when it does). If you drop a brick on your foot and break it, you've broken your foot, correct? You go to the doctor to get it checked out and reset, right?

"Why are you here?" the physician asks.

"I'm fine, doc," you respond.

My guess is that you would receive a strange reaction -- people typically go to the physician when something is wrong. In order to get help with the broken foot, you would need to tell the physician what happened and what you think the problem is. It is the same is with fear.

To eradicate fear's impact on your life—for it will circle back around and see if there is space for it—you have to recognize what it is and then decide to replace it with what

God has given you: the power of your voice to call into being the spirit of power, the spirit of love, and the spirit of a sound mind. (Just as we would call healing on the scene in the case of a broken foot.) Your authentic voice filled with God's power, His unfailing love, and His stability has the ability to transform your life from being one harassed by the spirit of fear into one that operates in power, love, and soundness of mind.

God has given each of us a voice. One that is to be authentic when exercised, when projected, when cast into the atmosphere with our words. Fear comes to get our words to be idle—going nowhere, doing nothing. It comes to get us to be quiet.

Let your authentic voice ring with power. God has given it to you, so use it and watch your world change!

The Pickup

This morning, I was in the kitchen reheating some soup when I noticed a green piece of paper on the floor. I thought it was from the bag I'd had the night before, and in my head, I said, "Londa, you missed the garbage can. Pick that up." When I got to the paper, I realized that it wasn't from the bag in which the soup mix had come; it was from something else. The colors were similar, but still, it was not from my bag. Then Holy Spirit gave me a quick nugget.

"Some people are like this: they go around picking up other people's things. Their problems. Their issues. Their insecurities. Their fears. Stop picking up other people's things. You have enough of your own to deal with."

Let me tell you, in that very moment, I saw how I had picked up some unhealthy things from others—whether or not they were offering them on purpose. Consciously and unconsciously, we process and store behaviors, attitudes, lifestyles, responses, actions, reactions, and more from others. They don't always appear overnight. Some may have taken time to manifest, yet they are there.

What have you picked up from others that you really don't need on your life's journey? Those things that will keep you in fear—feeling powerless, unloved, and unstable—and unable to passionately pursue your purpose?

- Have you picked up a bad temper?
- Have you picked up fear and insecurities?
- Have you picked up an unhealthy sense of importance? We are to think highly of ourselves but not more highly. There's a difference.
- Have you picked up bad eating habits?
- Have you picked up not eating because you are afraid to repeat a pattern? That's not a healthy pickup either.
- Have you picked up unhealthy relationship behavior? Are you staying in neglectful, abusive relationships, even friendships, because that is what you lived or saw in past times?

- Have you picked up reclusiveness?
- Have you picked up unhealthy family interactions?
- Have you picked up unhealthy parenting practices?
- Have you picked up an addiction that is affecting your ability to partner with God to carry out His plans and thoughts for your life?
- Have you picked up laziness?
- Have you picked up purpose-less living?

Today, decide that you are going to drop—right now and right here and right there—those things you picked up that aren't helping _____ e.g., you, your children, your family, your business or career, your relationships/friendships, and your future generations. Fill in the blank.

Let's—that is, you + me equaling "us"—choose to only pick up what we can use. When we are made aware of a pickup—for sometimes, we don't even know we've picked up something—let's assess it quickly and determine if it's of use to us.

The rest, if it comes in your path, put it in the garbage. That's its new residence—not you, not your mind, not your body, not your dreams, not your life visions, not your business, not your marriage, not your children, not your finances, not your home . . . not anything that is important to you.

Pick up life. It's for the living.

L.D. Robinson

9/22/22

#ThePickup #DontMissYourMoment

Power in Exchange for Fear

God offers us power in exchange for fear for a purpose: so that we live unfettered and unbound by anything other than Him. And even in that, He still offers freedom.

This power of which Paul speaks in 2 Timothy is not energy only. It is also *ability*. When we go to Ephesians, Chapter 1, Verses 15-22, we see this in confirmation.

New King James Version

15 Therefore I also, after I heard of your faith in the Lord Jesus and your love for all the saints, 16 do not cease to give thanks for you, making mention of you in my prayers: 17 that the God of our Lord Jesus Christ, the Father of glory, may give to you the spirit of wisdom and revelation in the knowledge of Him, 18 the eyes of your [f]understanding being enlightened; that you may know what is the hope of His calling, what are the riches of the glory of His inheritance in the saints, 19 and what is the exceeding greatness of His power toward us who believe, according to the working of His mighty power 20 which He worked in Christ when He raised Him from the dead and seated Him at His right hand in the heavenly places, 21 far above all principality [g] and [h]power and [i]might and dominion, and every name that is named, not only in this age but also in that which is to come.

22 And He put all things under His feet, and gave Him to be head over all things to the church, 23 which is His body, the fullness of Him who fills all in all.

Let us take a look at this from *The Voice* translation:

This has been copied as printed due to the emphasis made in the translation's text.

[15] This is why, when I heard of the faith in the Lord Jesus that is present in your community and of your great love for all God's people, [16] I haven't stopped thanking Him for

you. I am continually speaking to Him on your behalf in my prayers. *Here's what I say:*

[17] God of our Lord Jesus the Anointed, Father of Glory: *I call out to You on behalf of Your people.* Give them minds ready to receive wisdom and revelation so they will truly know You. [18] Open the eyes of their hearts, *and let the light of Your truth flood in.* Shine Your light on the hope You are calling them to embrace. Reveal to them the glorious riches You are preparing as their inheritance. [19] Let them see the full extent of Your power that is at work in those of us who believe, and may it be done according to Your might and power.

Friends, it is this same might and *resurrection* power that [20] He used in the Anointed One to raise Him from the dead and to position Him at His right hand in heaven. *There is nothing over Him.* [21] He's above all rule, authority, power, and dominion; over every name invoked, *over every title bestowed* in this age and the next. [22] God has placed all things beneath His feet and anointed Him as the head over all things for His church. [23] This church is His body, the fullness of the One who fills all in all.

Paul encourages the believers in Ephesus to acknowledge that they have been given the same power [energy and ability—thank you, Pastor Jerry M. Carter, Jr., for this] to live just like the resurrection power that raised Jesus from the dead. This power is what causes Him to live in triumph at God's own right hand, making intercession for us. Jesus not only has the ability to intercede for us, He has eternal energy to do so!

For what is Jesus making intercession? One thing for which He intercedes is that we receive the abundance of God's grace, energy, and ability so that our faith not fail us—that we complete our individual and collective [that is, the Church] our assignments in the earth.

You cannot be overtaken by fear and still complete your assignment! Jesus defeated fear so that we can have space for the power! God desires that we live *in* and live *out* this same power—defeating its presence and influence in our lives!

Read that again, please. I did not tell you that you cannot complete your assignment in the face of fear, but you have to refuse to be overtaken by it! Many times, we take the leap of faith even when we do not fully understand how we shall accomplish such a thing!

Remember, please, that the opposite of faith is *not* believing, doubting. Fear is a tagalong to that doubt. Many people have progressed, taken steps while fear *wanted* to overwhelm them. In fact, I have taken steps in obedience even when fear questioned, "How are you going to do *that*?" Well, when you take a step, you lessen the voice of fear. Each step increases the spirit of power in your life; you become emboldened by God's spirit of power maturing in your life.

You may be asking, "Well, L.D., all this is good, but how do I get rid of fear?"

Speak to it.

Speak to yourself.

Remember the power that you have been given and make a decision to exercise your authority.

Fill yourself up with God's Word and His thoughts.

Make steps—or leaps—to do the thing(s) that you know you should be doing, those things [actions, behaviors, habits, and more] that move you towards that which you know will cause you to experience your God-given, God-ordained curious work and life that He has designed *just for you.*

You have access to God's power. That power triumphs over fear . . . every single time.

Be not afraid. ***You do not have to be afraid.*** You do not have to live under the reign of fear, but you can operate in power and be all who you were created to be.

For God has not given us a spirit of fear, but of power and of love and of a sound mind. (2 Timothy 1:7)

A Confession of Power

I remind myself that God has not given to me the spirit of fear, but the spirit of power, and the spirit of love, and the spirit of a sound mind. I accept God's exchange for fear; I choose to operate in His power, His love, and His stability.

God has given to me His power so that I fulfill His plans, purposes, and thoughts for my life. His plans and thoughts are intentional for me according to Jeremiah 29:11.

I do not have to be afraid of what may come my way for He has told me that it is *all working together for my good because I love Him and am called according to His purpose* in Romans 8:28.

I do not have to be afraid because even that which has been unworkable must be joined to the workable power of God in my life and work out for my good.

I do not have to be afraid because God's spirit of love infuses my life to such a degree that fear cannot find a foothold in my mind or my thoughts.

I do not have to be afraid because James 1:17 tells me that *there is no variation or shadow of turning* in God. Because God is stable, I can be stable and of sound mind. I choose to operate in the spirit of a sound mind each day of my life. I am not double-minded because I use the power that I have been given to make sound choices.

I am a creature of great capacity. I have been created by God Himself, in the image and likeness of Him, His Son, and Holy Spirit.

God gives to me His energy and ability to be all I have been created to be and do all I have been created to do.

Fear has no place in my life in any way, shape, form, or activity.

I am free from fear. I am powerful. There is nothing that I cannot accomplish with God's spirit of power operating in me!

I will not miss my moment because of fear! I will be fully in each moment so that I can realize God's great plans and thoughts and purposes for me.

I am free! I am free! I am free!

Some Shorts

W*ritten in response to a story about a 67-year-old woman modeling a famous singer's clothing line*

For that person who's scared to start a new career . . . here's a reason to kick fear to the curb! When did it become okay to become so comfortable with fear and comfort that one is unwilling to risk it all for purpose, passion, and meaningful pursuit?

#NoFearHere
#ItWillHappen
#PutANewFearlessChapterInYourLifeBook

"This is what people get wrong: it is not that it was done without fear, but it was done out of greater love."

(Captain commenting on the great courage of Vietnam Veteran Melvin Morris when rescuing their sergeant's dead body while himself wounded and despite recommendations for the Medal of Honor, received a lesser honor)

Written a couple of weeks before my 40th birthday. Interestingly enough, this Unpinning Book 2 is releasing a few weeks before my 50th birthday

Every decade marks a new chapter. Indeed, each day turns the page in the book of one's life. As I approach forty in a few days, I stand amazed at God's grace and the keeping power that He's manifested in my life. I am excited about the next decade. I am excited about what is on the inside of me and all that will come out in the next ten years. I am on a mission to do what I have been created to do--leave an indelible mark in the earth for the cause of Christ. Look out, World!

Every leader must have a reservoir of perseverance. Your steadfastness is a direct tie to the realization of your vision. Even in the face of obstacles and past failures (those lessons that result from trying), your purposeful intent to accomplish your objectives will be the reason for your success.

#Perseverance

About the Author

L.D. Robinson is an author, publisher, website designer, and career consultant. A former IT and engineering consultant for almost two decades, her life took an unexpected turn which led to the writing and self-publishing of her first novel. Writing—and seeking out how to publish her book—led to the start of Ladero Press, a traditional Publishing Services Firm (PSF) in which she delights in helping make other authors' publication dreams come true.

While helping authors with projects during the past couple of years, L.D. found the need to establish a new venture, Pen to Press by Ladero, a Pay2Publish (TM) firm designed to assist authors and self-publishers through the publication process employing various levels of service based on client needs. Services are structured for single author and multiple author publications.

Additionally, L.D. is the owner of Ladero Design Works, a firm specializing in graphics design, website development, and social media. Ladero Design Works is a Wix Icon Partner.

L.D. is a firm believer in each person knowing and fulfilling their God-given purposes. She writes with a mission in mind—whether through fiction, nonfiction, or inspirational—and that is, "Don't Miss Your Moment!"

#DontMissYourMoment